You've Got RESPECTFUL Manners!

What to Say When You Don't Know How

Tactful Tips from A to Z
for Kids of All Ages

by Louise Elerding

You've Got RESPECTFUL Manners!
What to Say When You Don't Know How

Tactful Tips from A to Z
for Kids of All Ages

Written and Illustrated by Louise Elerding
Layout and Color Design by Bruce Gordon

Grandy Publications
Burbank, California

ISBN 13: 978-0-9729237-5-0
ISBN 10: 0-9729237-5-6
Library of Congress Control Number: 2007938136

Other books written by Louise Elerding:
You've Got Manners! Table Tips from A to Z for Kids of All Ages
Ya tienes buenos modales! Consejitos de A a Z Para ninos de todas edades
You've Got SOCIAL Manners ~ Party Pointers from A to Z for Kids of All Ages
The Art of Expression Through Fashion Feng Shui
Formulas For Dressing The Whole Person

To order additional books, call 800-326-8953 or e-mail MannersA2Z@aol.com
Visit us at www.youvegotmanners.com

Printed in China

Dedication

This book is dedicated to the memory of my Mother, Elmira "Myrto" Fleury, a true lady in every way. She repeatedly said to me as a child growing up, "Louise, be tactful." I had no idea what that meant at the time, but in hearing it over the years it created an appreciation for what I later recognized as being a gracious way to live.

Merci Maman!

Acknowledgments
(In A to Z Order)

Advisory Board: Alyssa, Amanda, Emily, Jason, and Tyler – my five brilliant grandchildren who gave me the key of "truth" for these pages.

Helen Leidner ~ a wonderful friend and role model in my life whose wisdom, tone, and timing are impeccable.

McSis's: Beverly McCord, Bonnie Brady Hoskins, and Marjorie Anderson ~ my heart sisters, who pondered, proofed, and added their insights to this topic.

Michael Vezo ~ the dependable and wise Advisor Extraordinaire, who I implore to always be in my publishing life.

Susie DeWeese ~ a Classy Chick who always supports, cheers, and makes time for a "teacher's review" of this galley sheet.

Treasured Family ~ Alyson, Kristin, Tom, and Augie – a continual source of pride, fun, and confirmation of who my life's blessings truly are.

TACTFUL TIPS
from A to Z

tact·ful (takt'fel) *adj.* having a keen sense of what to say or do to avoid giving offense.

re·spect·ful (re spek'fel) *adj.* showing politeness and concern for another.

There are times when something happens, and a person just does not know what to say. It could be because they are scared, sad, embarrassed, angry, or uncomfortable for some reason. If so, they freeze up and don't say anything at all. Often, saying the right words helps everyone feel better.

What do you say when you don't know how to say it?

You can say anything to anyone if you keep this in mind: "Tone and timing is everything!" Helen Leidner, a special friend of mine, taught me this valuable saying. What this means is that if you speak from your heart with goodness and respect for the other person, and use tact – the *tone* of your voice will be kind, and you will choose just the right *time* to tell them.

Being tactful means telling someone how you feel while still being truthful, and without making anyone wrong. It makes the world a considerate and peaceful place.

Hello!

We are Polly Politely and Milton Manners here to help you with ways of speaking to others when you are not sure of what to say.

We've invited our cousins Tyler Tactful, Amanda Mannerly, and Alyssa Appropriate here to help us come up with easy ways to say difficult things.

Being respectful and tactful when talking to people is another way of having good manners.

Come along with us now as we take a look at how you can say anything to anybody – and make it truthful AND kind at the same time.

ASKING for permission shows respect to other people. When you want to borrow anything, use something, or occupy someone else's space, just ask. It can't hurt! If they say "yes," Hooray! If they say "no," that's OK, too. Don't take it personally - it just didn't work out this time. Here is an example of what you could say:

"Mrs. Seymour, may I please play a video game on your computer while I wait for my Mom to come pick me up?"

APOLOGIES take courage. Be the brave one and apologize when you've done something you are sorry about.

"I want to tell you that I am sorry for breaking your window. I will watch where I toss the ball from now on."

BAD LANGUAGE is not invited to any gathering. When someone uses bad words, its OK to say:

"Bad words are not 'cool' here. Keep it clean, please."

BULLYING is a sign of <u>weakness</u>. The kids who bully are pretending to be BIG – but they are not big at all. Show them by your example how to be a winner in life and a person of strong character. Do not react to anything they say or do.

"Let it go. There is no time for this kind of acting out."

If you are CAUGHT CHEATING at anything, own up with no excuses and apologize. Don't deny it – that's making two mistakes! You can say something like:

"I know I was not supposed to do that. May I have a second chance to make it right?"

CUTTING in line is sort of like stealing. It is taking a space that really does not belong to you. It's OK to speak up to the person cutting in, while wearing your smile:

"This is the line, and we have been waiting our turn for a long time. Would you please take your place at the end? Thanks."

To DISAGREE with someone is healthy. Doing it in a friendly tone of voice and with a nice attitude is what makes the difference. Sharing opinions with a smile can help make new friends, not enemies.

"Danny, do you really want Sara to win our school election? I have a different opinion and I think John will do the best job. We have very different points of view, but either way — we are all friends in the end."

People with DISABILITIES don't want to be left out. They like to talk about a lot of the same things you do. Start a conversation with a handicapped person, and anyone who is disabled and participating in your group.

"Hi. How do you like this cooking class so far? I noticed you have your leg in a brace. What happened? If you need help carrying the baking tools to the next station, let me know."

EMBARRASSMENT usually leaves us feeling weird and not knowing what to say. Once you talk about it – that funny feeling can go away. Other kids have been embarrassed about something, sometime, so they will understand.

"I feel so embarrassed because I started to cry on the playground when some kids were bullying me." P.S. Crying is good. It's reminding all of us that we each have real feelings.

EVERY person is going to die one day. When someone close and special to you passes away it is very difficult. Talking about the death of a friend or someone you love helps the healing. Don't be afraid to talk about the deceased person. You may start by asking a question or saying something kind:

"How are you doing since the funeral? I really liked your brother a lot. He was always my hero. He helped me and so many kids learn how to be good Eagle Scouts. We're all going to really miss him."

FIXING anything personal for someone that can be done on the spot is OK to do. You are doing them a big favor, so don't be shy about telling them when something can be fixed. For example:

"I thought you'd want to know you have some spinach caught in your braces," or "Your blouse is unbuttoned." or "There's dust on your coat; want some help brushing it off?"

FAMILY divorce makes many people sad. If someone you know is going through this, you can tell them:

"I am feeling badly for you now. This must be really hard for you. When you feel like it, let's talk."

GOSSIP is talking behind someone's back . It can be true or untrue, but either way it can hurt people. If someone is spreading gossip, just say:

"Danny is my friend, just like you are my friend, and I wouldn't let anyone spread rumors about you. So, let's stop talking about Danny."

GREET whomever opens the door to the house you are visiting, with a nice smile and friendly words. It might be your friend's parents, other adults, or a teacher. Look them right in the eye, introduce yourself, and ask something about them too:

"Hi. It's me, _____ . I picked some flowers for you from my garden. How is your vegetable patch doing so far this season?"

HOUSE rules need to be respected. If you don't know a certain house rule while visiting in someone's home, and they scold you, just be brave and calm and say:

"I am sorry I ate potato chips in the living room, but I did not know that was your house rule. I won't do that again." Or you may want to tell your friend: "Bobby, the rule in our house is 'no baseball hats at the dinner table.' You can put yours here on the bench with mine."

HUNGER pains can make you want to roar like a lion. What if you feel funny asking for something to eat while you are in someone else's house?

First of all, always try to have a snack before you go to someone's home, so that you don't expect them to feed you right away. Try to have a snack in your pocket or backpack too. But if you just HAVE to eat, politely say:

" Mrs. Moore, I feel funny asking you this, but is there something I could eat right now, just to hold me over until dinner? I am feeling painfully hungry. Thanks!"

13

INTRODUCTIONS by kids to adults has an easy rule: Always say the name of the adult, or the person of special importance first. It sounds like this:

"Aunt Janet, this is my friend Cami.", "Coach Jim, this is my brother Jordan."

INVITATIONS are a compliment to you. Someone wants you with them. Answer them as soon as possible. If you can't be there, be truthful about the reason. Making up a fib when you don't want to go can backfire on you and is not necessary. You can be honest by saying:

"I am so sorry. I have already made other plans for that day" or "I wish I could be there, but I can't this time. Can we do something together next week?"

JUSTICE FOR ALL ... are words you've heard before. Be as fair as you can at all times. When someone is being unfair to you, stand up for your rights and the rights of your friends. You are the BIG ONE when you are fair-minded.

"It is not fair that you took three party favors, because now there aren't enough to go around for everyone who was supposed to get one. Would you please put two back?"

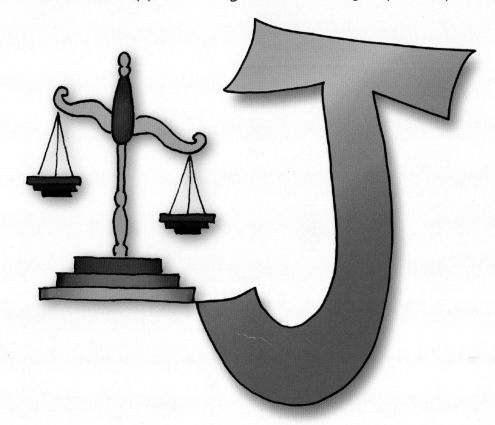

JEALOUSY sometimes makes us feel weird, and we act grumpy. If your friend got picked for the team and you didn't ... you could say:

"Colin, I was pretty disappointed when I didn't get picked for the team and you did, so I was acting out – but I'm really glad for you & I hope you have a good game."

15

KEEPING a secret is something that good friends do for each other. Be the buddy that your friends can count on not to 'blab' what they told you in confidence.

"Emily, you asked me not to tell anyone your secret – and I promise you that I won't." If someone wants you to reveal a secret, say " Sandy, I wouldn't tell your secret to anyone if you asked me not to, so please understand that I can't tell you Nick's secret now."

There may be time when you are told some dangerous information as a secret. In this case you may say, "I can't keep a dangerous secret. We should tell an adult."

KINDNESS to older people says a lot about your "heart." Never be shy or afraid to talk with older people, relatives, and friends who are in a special home or hospital. It cheers up their day SO much just to have you go up to them, smile and say something nice.

"Hello Great-Grandmother. The flowers you put on your windowsill look really pretty. I like poppies too. My class is planting a flower and vegetable garden in the school's side-yard next month. I'll bring a surprise from that garden later."

LYING gets you into all sorts of trouble ... sooner or later! Remember ... always tell the truth – it's the easiest to remember!

Once people know you lie – they will never trust you or believe you again.

"Sometimes I feel like lying, but I always know that I'll be better off when I tell the truth."

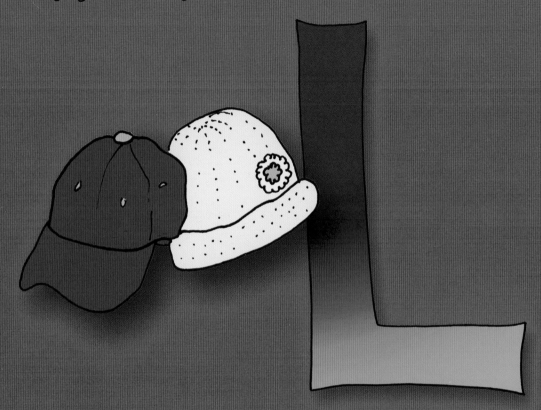

LOSS of hair because of chemotherapy or any illness makes some people feel very different and self-conscious. Say something to help them feel better:

"Jessica, that's a cute looking cap you're wearing – and it's a great color on you!" –or–
"My cousin went through what you are, and I know how he felt. You still look good to us.
Hey – want to be on our spelling team tomorrow?"

MISPRONOUNCING a name happens. Sometimes a teacher or a new friend calls you by another name by mistake. It's OK to smile and politely say:

"Ms. Silva, my name isn't Taylor, it's Tyler."

MESSAGES that you take over the phone can get mixed-up. Even though we try to be correct, sometimes we goof. If you get confused, take your time, and ask for more help. It's better to slow down and have the message repeated:

"I want to be sure to get this message right, and I don't think I have everything you said written down. Would you please go over it once again with me? Thanks a lot."

NOISES like burping sound un-cool. If you hear that noise, just ignore it and look the other way – no laughing or giving it extra attention. If it's you that made that sound, then quickly apologize and talk about something better!

"Excuse me. By the way, did you know that our P.E. coach is taking our class to the high school tennis tournament next month because we did so well in our league?"

NEWCOMERS to your classroom or your neighborhood will welcome a friendly face. Be the one to go up to them first – be a helpful new buddy. If YOU are the newcomer and no one comes up to you, find one person who looks at you, then smile and say:

"Hi. I'm new here. I saw you up in front of the room. Do you want to eat lunch in the cafeteria together today?"

If you are **OVERWEIGHT** or underweight and someone makes a rude comment about your appearance, remember that good people come in all sizes. Be confident and calmly say:

"Words like that 'sting'. Let's be kind to each other, so please try to say something nice – and I will do the same for you."

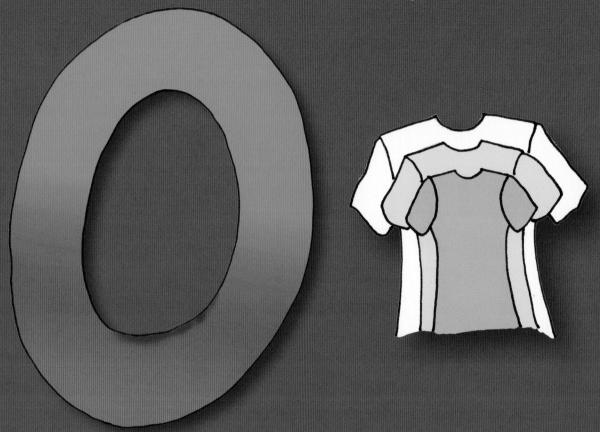

OTHER races, religions, and cultures deserve our respect. The more we read and learn about how other people live, the more educated and understanding we can be about our differences. If you hear a slur or a bigoted remark, do not join in. Stand up for equality.

"Danny – there's no place for talk like that here."

PRIVACY is your right. If you need to be alone for a good reason,
then you can always say in a nice tone:

"Grandma, I'd rather change my clothes in private right now; thanks."
Or, "Jason, can you wait out in the hall while I talk with my teacher about my test? "

When **PETS** pass away it's a very sad time. Telling your friends that you are sorry is very caring.
Don't be afraid to bring it up. If they don't feel like talking about it then,
at least they know you care.

"Amanda, I heard that Rusty died. He was the best dog. I really feel sad for you.
I have a picture of him at the beach last summer. Would like to have it?"

QUESTIONS that people might ask you that are of a very personal matter do not have to be answered. Never feel that just because someone asks you those questions that it means you have to answer them. It is your privilege to say:

"This is a personal matter for me – it's something I don't talk about outside of my family. I hope you understand."

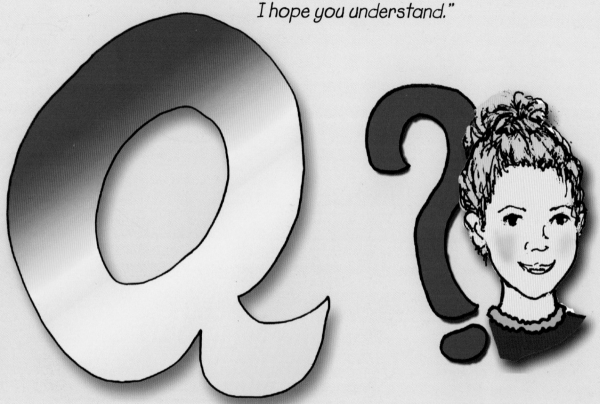

QUARRELING sometimes clears the air of something that needs to be talked about. Say what is bothering you without making the other person wrong, and then try to make up and be nice to each other.

"Sean, I was really angry when you didn't show up at the meeting like you promised yesterday. I had to haul all of the boxes by myself. Please call me from now on if you can't be there. OK?"

RUDE people can make us angry sometimes. Remember that the rude person is the one who has to learn HIS manners! You know your good manners, so don't let his bad ones rub off on you. If someone says something rude, answer something nice with a smile, and move on. Stay happy!

"Easy Buddy ... let's all have a good day."

If you RECEIVE a gift that you don't like or want, be nice in what you say.
You can be honest and kind at the same time:

"Auntie, thanks for these new mittens. It was nice of you to bring me a souvenir from your trip."

SPECIAL or STRUGGLING students who are not as quick in math or reading as most of the class need your understanding. Show your kindness by boosting and cheering them on to do the best they can. Avoid any teasing or snickering.

"Robbie, when you read out loud in class today, I could understand everything you said. Good job."

SIMPLE compliments put a smile on a person's face and can make them happy for the whole day. Saying something nice spreads good cheer. Give everyone you see today one nice greeting:

"Nice jacket!" – "Awesome science project you did!" – "Cool shoes !" – "Great speech you gave this morning !"

TIME limits on the phone, or online on a shared computer, gives everyone a turn to make their calls. Be the fair one, and suggest:

"I need to make some calls too – so could we pick a time limit of 10 minutes each, then we'll all get a chance to make our calls. "~or~ "Sure, you go ahead and make your calls, and I'll be waiting next in the line-up. Is the 10-minute time limit OK with you?"

THANK YOU notes are like a super mini-gift. The person receiving them feels happy in getting a surprise in the mail. If you're the person sending them ~ give yourself a pat-on-the-back for going the extra mile. Write notes when you want to show very sincere appreciation for something. Try to make at least 2 or 3 sentences. You could write:

"Dear Grandpa, The savings bond you gave me for my birthday is great. I like watching it grow every year. Thanks a lot for this big gift and teaching me how to save money. Love, Alyssa"

USING Sign Language is a way of talking. If you notice someone 'signing', and you want to say something to that person...don't hang back. Go up to them. One of you might even have a pencil and paper. The two of you will figure out how to communicate together and have fun . Say:

"I see you are using Sign Language. Do you read lips too? I'd like to say something to you."

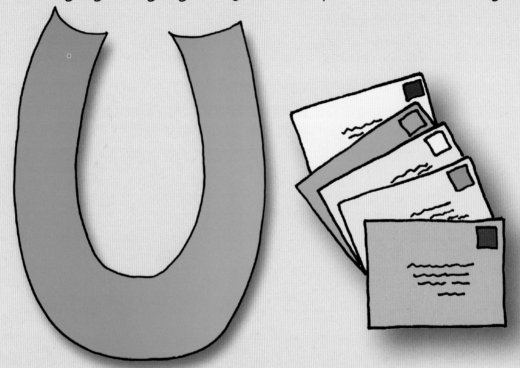

UNDERSTAND that some parties have to limit the number of people that are invited. If you find out that you have not been invited to a special party, and wonder why you were left out, don't guess that it was because they don't like you. Lots of people like you very much.
Maybe this party was in a room with limited space, or a limited budget.
If someone asks about you and the party, you can say:

"No, I was not invited to Chelsea's party this time, and it's OK.
She and I both like riding horses, and we will see each other at the stables next week."

VICTORY is so sweet! When your team wins, remember to thank everyone who was a part of that event. Never take all the credit.

"Hey guys ... each one of you did something to make us all winners today. We won together!"

VOICES heard inside the theater while watching a movie or a play can be such a distraction. Be a 'Silent Sam' and be a good example. People talking too loud or goofing around may not know how noisy they sound. If it doesn't stop, call an usher, or nicely ask:

"I am having trouble hearing the program. Would you mind not talking until it's over. Thanks."

When you are **WRONGLY** accused of doing something you did NOT do ... it feels awful.
Sometimes it's by a teacher, a relative, or even a stranger. In a calm and positive way, say:

"I need to tell you that I did not do what you said. It's important to me that you know the truth. There is a mistake here and I would like you to hear what really happened."

WHEELCHAIRS have special passengers riding in them. Don't stand back –
go up and talk to the person like you do with all of your other friends.
You can even offer to push them to where you are going next:

"Hi! Would you like me to push you to class? At recess I'm going out to the soccer field to cheer on the game. I could push you there if you want to come along."

XYZ means "examine your zipper." It's a helpful way of saving a person embarrassment about a pant zipper being down – and doing it in a fun and laughing way.

"Hey Justin – XYZ."

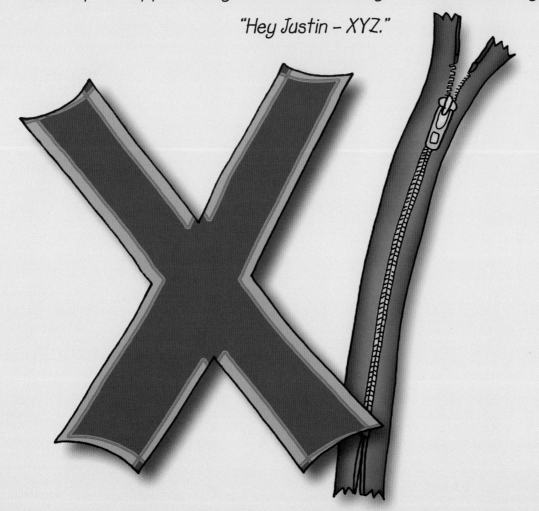

"X-CUSE me" helps the bruise feel better. If you bump into someone, always say "Excuse me" – even if it happened so fast that you're not sure who bumped into whom. This is a nice way to let the person know it was an accident and not done on purpose.

"Excuse me – I hope you're not hurt."

YOUNGER brothers and sisters like doing what the bigger kids are doing. It might seem pesty to you now, but you were their age once. Try to be nice to your siblings when you have friends over and work out a plan that makes everyone happy. Maybe it sounds like this:

"Mindy and Matt, how about you play this game with us now, then you can play with your own puzzles while Jason and I build this tricky wood tower."

YOUR report card is personal and belongs to you. You can share as little or as much about your grades as you want to. If you didn't do too well and you feel disappointed or self conscious, you do not have to tell anyone about it – even if they ask.

"I'm taking my report card home first – my Mom wants to be the first one to see it."

ZERO points in the card game of 'Hearts' means you are a winner. Zero points in a basketball game means you've lost. Be a happy-humble-winner and a good-sport-loser. When someone loses, you can say to them (or yourself!) :

"You did your best – and the other team was just ready for a win. You'll have your time to win soon."

ZIG -ZAG your social conversations. That means go "back and forth," letting everyone have a chance to get their opinion voiced. No one likes a "dominator" - a person who takes over, interrupts others while they are in the middle of a sentence, and talks non-stop. Be polite and take a breath in-between thoughts and hear what someone else has to say.

"I just went to Walt Disney World and I went on so many rides. Have any of you been there? (pause) My favorite area was Adventureland. What did you like?" (listen)

Certificate of Special Achievement

HEAR ME NOW

_____

(Your Name)

I know my Tactful Tips from A to Z

and

I'VE GOT RESPECTFUL MANNERS!

Join "The Polite Team of the World"

Your one-time membership fee is only $5.00

With membership you will receive:

A complimentary deck of "Pass The Manners, Please!" cards ($9.99 value).

Your name posted on our YOUVEGOTMANNERS.COM website as an
Official Member of "The Polite Team of the World."

A 25% discount on the purchase of any "You've Got Manners" books or cards
listed on pages 38 and 39.

To become a member, send an e-mail to: MannersA2Z@aol.com

In the subject line, enter "Polite Team Membership."

Write your name, age, and the state where you live.

Write one favorite manner you like to use.

To pay by credit card: include card number, 3 digit code on back, expiration date,
name on card, full mailing address, and phone number.

Or to pay by mail, please call 1-800-326-8953 to hear where to send your payment.

Welcome!   It's great to have you on board.

How it all began ...

You've Got Manners Enterprises began with a family road trip – a 1,000 mile vacation through Canada the summer of 2002.

To pass the time among our three generations in a mini-van, the game of naming and playing with table manner ideas became our car activity and then a book.

Soon after the first book on "Table Tips" was published, a series evolved—looking at all types of manners that kids come in contact with, such as social, school time, and how to say things with kindness and truth.

Pictured here is the Five Member Advisory Board for YGM Enterprises, who inspires this venture, with the author Louise Elerding—referred to as "Grandy" by her five sensational grandkids.

Their quarterly Board meetings are generating ideas and decisions for the future, while seeing all possibilities through the eyes of "kids."

ABOVE: **The Advisory Board.**
Front row, left to right: Emily, Louise, Alyssa, Amanda.
Back row, left to right: Jason, Tyler.

About Louise Elerding

Louise Elerding, AICI, CIP is a Personal Appearance Coach, author, speaker, Image industry trainer, Fashion Feng Shui Facilitator/Trainer, and owner of Professional Image Partners at The Color Studio in Burbank, California, since 1983.

Individuals, businesses, and groups employ Louise to align their inner strengths with their outward appearance – from personal issues to company branding.

Louise is a charter member of the Association of Image Consultants International, AICI, having served an International President 1996-97. She received the esteemed 1999 Award of Excellence from AICI for her contributions to this worldwide industry organization.

In 2001 she was inducted into the International Who's Who of Professional & Business Women's HALL of FAME.

Louise has been quoted in numerous books, articles, publications, among them: *Parenting Magazine, Redbook, Glamour Magazine, L.A. Business Journal, Maximum Style-Rodale Press*, the *Chicago Tribune, Baltimore Sun, Pacific Sun, One World Live, CNN.com*. Louise also appears on local cable television and writes a monthly newspaper column entitled "Pass The Manners, Please".

Along with these books, her Table Manners teaching curriculum is being taught across the country.

Speak your best words with perfect tone and timing!

We want you along!
Be a part of the Polite Team of the World.

For information regarding Manners classes, please call 1-800-326-8953.

To find an instructor — an OMM (Official Manners Messenger) — in your area, visit our website

www.youvegotmanners.com

INDEX

You've Got Manners! Series

You've Got Manners!
Table Tips from A to Z for Kids of All Ages

¡Ya tienes buenos modales!
Consejitos de A a Z Para ninos de todas edades

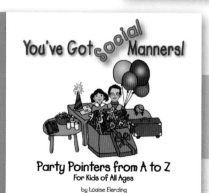

You've Got SOCIAL Manners!
Party Pointers from A to Z for Kids of All Ages

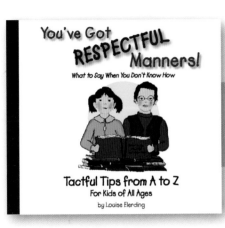

You've Got RESPECTFUL Manners!
Tactful Tips from A to Z for Kids of All Ages

"Pass the Manners, Please" Card Deck
It's Flashcards and a Rummy Game for the Entire Family

See you later, and hooray for you
as you speak confidently with truth and kindness!